My Story of Grace: A Self-Reflection Handbook

By
Dr. Edyth E. Young

ACKNOWLEDGMENT

I would first and foremost love to give God all the honor, praise, and thanksgiving for his everlasting love and his marvelous free gift of grace that has sustain me through my journey of life with his right hand of righteousness. I am eternally grateful to God for inspiring me with every word and every Bible scripture he has poured into my spirit for authoring <u>My Story of Grace: A Self-Reflection Handbook.</u> I am in awe of God's presence when I write. I am beyond grateful to sit in his presence as I reflect on my life to put my story of mercy, grace, love and faith in writing to share with others, and give them a crystal-clear vision of the glorious plan for all of humanity to live the abundant beautiful life our Heavenly Father has for each individual's journey of life.

I would like to also acknowledge my parents, sisters, grandparents, aunts, uncles, nieces, nephews, cousins, and friends for the impactful role they have all had in my life. All of my family and friends are the *rich picturesque tapestry that makes me uniquely me*, and I will always value and appreciate their support and encouragement that has helped me in all my endeavors and achievements including authoring this book.

It cannot go without saying how appreciative and grateful I am for the superior guidance and outstanding support of my publisher.

To,

The Publisher,

I give you a heartfelt thank you for helping me get <u>My Story of Grace: A Self-Reflection Handbook</u> ready to share with my readers globally.

DEDICATION

This book is dedicated to the memory of my (Sister Cuz) Barbara Thompson who died from COVID-19 April 11, 2020, one day before Easter the day of Resurrection of our Lord and Savior Jesus Christ. Barbara was and still is an anchor of wisdom and courage in my heart. I feel in creditably blessed to have had her as my first cousin and how we grew up like sisters. Her father and my mother are siblings. Even though Sister Cuz was just two years older than me, she taught me so many life lessons about walking in courage and faith, living life to the fullest, and how to pray to God in a spirit of humility. Sister Cuz, I will always hold you in my heart and all the lovely lessons you taught me. Until we meet again in Glory, my loving and beautiful Sister Cuz.

In addition, this book is dedicated to all the people around the world (Our International Interconnection Brotherhood of Humanity) who have been impacted by the COVID-19 Pandemic. My heart goes out to all of you, and I pray that each of you will have the comfort you need. God is still comforting my heart every day from the loss of my Sister Cuz from COVID-19 on April 11, 2020.

ABOUT THE AUTHOR

Dr. Edyth E. Young is a certified reading diagnostician, curriculum developer, professional development coach and educational evaluator. Her educational and professional experiences are broad and enriched in scope. She holds a B.A. in Early Childhood and Elementary Education (Illinois Type 03, K-9 License) from Northeastern University; an M.A. in Elementary Education Curriculum Development and Supervision from the University of Iowa; and a Ph.D. in Reading Research and Educational Evaluation from the University of Illinois at Champaign-Urbana. She also holds an Illinois Type 10 Reading Specialist and Administrative Reading Specialist License.

After three plus decades of being an educator and moving close to my retirement, I prayed and asked God what would he have me do after retirement. I did not want to wait until after I retired. I wanted to start my ministry in the things God has plan for me to do in the next part of my journey of life. First, God call me to the ministry in June of 2021. I became a Licensed Ordain Minister, and God placed in my heart the service of Chaplaincy. Therefore, I started my studies in the Master of Chaplaincy Seminary. This seminary was amazing. I learned to grasp all the diverse types of Chaplaincies and the significant purpose of chaplains in God's plans for reaching souls with extreme compassion. I had to have an in-depth knowledge of seven key types of Chaplains. It was extraordinary for me to feel deep in my heart the divine call of God to be a Hospice Chaplain. In listening to God concerning his plan for me to be a Hospice Chaplain, I enrolled and trained at The Hospice Chaplaincy Institute, and after much training and application experiences, I received my certification as a Hospice Chaplain. I am currently continuing my Chaplaincy ministry education for my National

Chaplaincy license with Christian Leaders and Christian Leaders Alliance.

Table of Contents

INTRODUCTION

What is God's grace? The first thing that comes to my mind to answer the question is grace is the free favor of God. In In this book, <u>My Story of Grace: A Self-Reflection Handbook</u>, I would like to take you on a journey with me to look at the glorious power of God's grace, and how he wants to freely surround our life here on Earth with his marvelous gift of Grace. On this journey, we will closely examine the unmerited favor of God's grace.

I will always use the lower-case g letter when I am speaking about God's grace. On the other hand, I will always use the upper-case G when I am speaking about Grace my personified very dear life-long friend and my guardian angel. As I travel through my journey of life, Grace is always with me at every turn. It is my greatest desire that we can all reflect, learn, and apply our understanding of God's amazing grace through my dear friend and personal guide, Grace. She is the personification of God's amazing grace that is so freely offered to all. I want every reader of <u>My Story of Grace</u> to take away valuable lessons about God's amazing grace and love. I pray that every reader will celebrate their own personal, free, unmerited favor of God's grace. The journey begins.

CHAPTER ONE

For I Know the Plans I Have for You Declares the Lord
(Jeremiah 29:11) NIV Bible

On October 8, 1960, I was born into this world, and I received the same loving stamp of grace from the declaration of God in Jeremiah 29:11 over me and all born before me, and all born after me. In the New International Version (NIV) Bible, Jeremiah 29:11 is an undeniably amazing declaration from God to all humanity around the entire world. Let us take a detailed look at every phrase of Jeremiah 29:11. The verse states, **"For I know the plans I have for you declares the Lord, plans to prosper you and not to harm you, plans to give you hope and a future."** The first phrase reveals to us that God Almighty has a plan for everyone. We all have the gift of God's plan for us. So, let us draw near to God to know our individual plan for our journey and mission for life.

Once you know your personal plan from God, stick to his plan. Walk in God's personal plan for you joyously and meticulously; that plan is your personal gift of greatness. As an educational researcher, reading specialist, and diagnostician, I have treated hundreds of students with learning disabilities and dyslexia, and in every case and every diagnostic profile, I have always discovered something they are excellent at and have a passion for in their personal life, and that is their personal seed of greatness. I am a firm believer that we all have a seed of greatness that God made in his declaration to humanity and that he knows the plan he has for everyone. Therefore, when we truly recognize God's plan for us and the gift of his grace, we will begin to recognize how this gift is wrapped up as our beautiful seed of greatness. It is especially important to accept God's gift of grace.

We cannot just stop at accepting the gift of God's grace, and our own personal seed of greatness. We need to embrace it as our journey of life passion and mission. In order for our seed of greatness gift to flourish and prosper, we must cultivate and grow that seed, that special gift that you are really great at or something that you really care about, to make a positive change in your life and the life of others. Please read the Parable of the Mustard Seed that Jesus taught in Matthew 13:31-32 and compare it to your seed of greatness that has freely been given to you through God's gift of grace and his plan that he has decreed over your life. God is the Master Builder, and we are his masterpiece.

God will never steer you off the plan he has for you. In my early childhood years, I can clearly remember like it was yesterday being asked the question, "What do you want to be when you grow up?" I am sure all over the world, young children are asked the same question as well as telling grown-ups all the different things they think they want to be. It is an exciting time of wonder, fun, and imagination in the life of a young child. God's plan for the free, unmerited favor of his grace is for all humanity to come to the awareness of his Central Plan for each individual's life journey. Think of it as what you will be when you grow up under God's Central Plan he declared for you in Jeremiah 29:11.

The first time I experienced my miraculous gift of God's grace and favor was when I was just two months old, and that was the moment that I believe my dear lifelong friend Grace my guardian angel became my guide on my journey of life and to help me as I live out the plan God declared for me. I am sure you are wondering how a two-month-old infant could have a miraculous encounter with God and her guardian angel. Well, you see, I was not aware, because I was just an infant. It was about what happened to me and the pain my parents experienced. They are the primary source who told me what happened to me at two months of age, and their account is forever in my memory. Okay, here is what happened when I was two months old: I became extremely sick, and my parents took me to the hospital as soon as possible. When my parents got me to the hospital, the doctors told my parents that I had Chicken Pox, pneumonia, a severe asthma attack that was hindering my breathing, and a fever of 103 and climbing.

My parents told me that the doctors put me into an isolated room with mist dropping 24/7 and oxygen pumping through my tiny little body in an effort to keep me alive. My parents could not come into the room to hold me or even touch me, and that broke their hearts. All they could do was look through the window at me in isolation all by myself. They had a great deal of fear, wondering how their little baby girl could live with Chicken Pox, pneumonia, and a severe asthma attack that was hindering her breathing and an extremely high fever. They told me that they had feelings that I could die. However, they did not realize at the time that I was not in that isolated room by myself. God stepped in with mercy and his loving grace to sustain my little life; it was a miracle! God knew his plan for me and my gift of greatness and my life purpose he degreed over me. I am so happy that, as an infant, I experienced the majestic power of the almighty God. He said that I would live and not die. The favor/grace of God was shining down on my tiny little body. I thank God that my parents made sure that I knew my *Story of Grace* and the miracle of life that was given to me. Now, as I grew older, around the ages of 5 to 12 years of age, my mother rushed me to the Cook County Hospital Emergency Room in Chicago at least two-to-three times a week with severe asthma attacks. It was so profound how the love, and mercy of God's grace and my Guide Grace were right there with me at every turn. To this day, I can personally still remember and visualize those high-speed rushes to the hospital. After the Chicago police pulled my mother over the very first time and saw my mother's desperate despair, he looked over at me, desperately trying to breathe, and heard the sound of my whizzing like a large orchestra band.

The police quickly jumped in front of my mother's car and gave us a faster police escort to the hospital right to the Emergency Room door, and the doctors and nurses were right there, ready to take care of me immediately. Most of the time, the doctors and the nurses could stabilize me, and I was able to go home, but the weekly cycle of the two-to-three trips each week to the Emergency Room continued. The hospital trips were so frequent that the police knew why my mother was speeding, and they would always get in front of her car to give us a police escort right to the Emergency Room. However, there were times that I had to be hospitalized, and some of those times, I had to be placed in the Intensive Care Unit inside an oxygen tent like the one you see here in the picture.

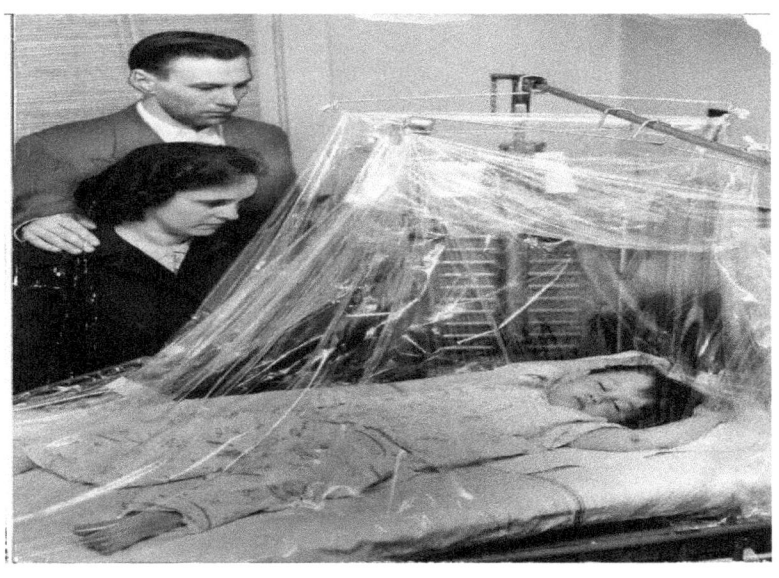

To this very day, I genuinely believe that I am alive because of God's amazing grace, my guardian angel Grace, my dear mother's close monitoring over me and teaching me how to monitor my asthma in addition to the Chicago Police that would always give my mother and me a safe escort to the Emergency Room like Angels of Mercy. My life-long guide Grace was always there with me guiding me under God's amazing blessings of favor to keep me alive. Even at an early age, I knew that God was watching over me, and I loved him so much as I still do love him today and forever more.

At the end of each chapter, I would like my readers to pause and reflect on the chapter, and journal your experience of God's grace as it relates to each chapter, which comes from a Bible verse. This reflective time at the end of each chapter will help you reflect on the lessons you personally learned and to connect to God's amazing grace through self-reflection

Happy reflections and exploring <u>Your Story of Grace</u>.

Reflections and Lessons Learned in Chapter One

CHAPTER TWO

For This, God is Our God Forever: He Will Be Our Guide
to the Very End (Psalm 48:14) NIV Bible

Have you ever had to drive somewhere, but you had no idea how to get there, and you had a feeling of unease because you did not want to get lost? I sure have been in that situation many times, and maybe you have been, too. I wish I had my own personal driving guide. I am sure you can remember back in the day using paper foldup maps when we were driving on a trip with family or friends. Remember the many calls we made to places where we were trying to get directions or using our computer to get good old MapQuest directions to guide us to our destination? Today, we have moved to navigational systems in our cars to be a guide for us along the way, and we all know about Siri on our phones. All we have to do is ask Siri for directions from one address to another address, and Siri will guide us right to our destination while talking to us as she guides us to wherever we need to go. Wow, what an evolution in travel guidance. We really can celebrate the technological improvements to get us to our desired destinations.

Now, let us take a look at the Greatest Navigational Guide for our journey of life. God's amazing grace is the greatest navigational force we could ever imagine. Remember the Bible verse for this chapter: For this God is our God forever. He will be our guide to the very end. (Psalm 48:14 NIV Bible) Think about God's amazing promise to be our guide through every twist and turn in our lives. This promise is so especially important to me because here is where my lifelong guide, Grace, the personification of God's grace and my dear guardian angel shows up repeatedly to guide me with the loving hand of God's mercy and grace. I have had many tears, sorrows, and disappointments. However, I have always believed, and I will always believe, that God has a plan for me and that his everlasting love and Grace my guardian angel will keep me steadfast and unmovable in my faith. Psalm 38:8 (KJV) gives us a deep assurance when we read the words of God speaking to us to let us know unequivocally that he knows the right paths for us and that he will instruct us and guide us with his eye. I personally find great comfort in the promise of God in Psalm 38:8 (KJV) that he will always be our all-powerful navigational guide and teacher through *everything* we face in life. God will *always keep his promise*, because he truly is our kind and loving Heavenly Father who personally knows everything about each of us, and he wants only the absolute best for his *beloved children,* and we are the children of God. Therefore, *imagine* resting your head in God's arms or holding his hand with all your heart, trust, and love, knowing that you are in the Father's Hand and the spirit of comfort wraps you up in a state of peace.

When I was 17, 18, 19, and in my early twenties, my church friends would call me Job from the Bible because Job went through unimaginable pain and loss. However, Job would never give up; he was always resolved that God was his guide and redeemer. In Job's latter years, the Almighty God opened up the windows of heaven and poured out blessings on Job. God's blessings to Job were much greater than all the things he lost. So, you see, my church friends called me Job because they knew unequivocally the challenging times and heartbreaking experiences I was going through.

My friends strongly believed that God was my guide from the beginning to the end, and just like Job, God was going to be my guide, and he would open up the heavens and pour out blessings over my life. One thing I would always do, and I still do to this very day, is to ask God to be my guide and to please grant me his grace and mercy. I genuinely believe that God answers that prayer for grace and mercy every day of my life, and my lifelong friend and guardian angel Grace guides me through my valleys and my mountain tops. God took all of those mammoth disappointments, tears, and sorrows when I was 17, 18, 19, and early twenties, and washed them all away. The Almighty God stepped in and, opened up the heavens and poured out blessings and comfort over my mind, body, and soul. Well, my church friends and I could not imagine how God, the Greatest Navigational Guide, and Grace, my life-long guardian angel and companion would turn my navigational system in a totally different direction.

The Almighty God, who is the Greatest Navigator, absolutely put me on a splendiferous path for my life journey. God took all those painful disappointments of my late teens and early 20s and totally turned my life's navigational system to redirect my path to my gift and seed of greatness he decreed over my life in the Bible verse Jeremiah 29:11. However, I want you to know from the core of my heart and soul as I went through those periods of devastation and disappointments God and my Guide Grace were both there guiding me with such a heavenly realm of comfort. I really felt God's grace, and peace. I also felt my beloved guardian angel Grace standing right by my side in the heavenly realm of comfort and peace. I want to share that heavenly realm of comfort and peace I experienced with everyone.

You see, we must hold firm to God's unchanging hand when we are going through troubling waters and the storms of life. Think with me for a moment and let us look at the phrase *going through*; instead of feeling down when we say, "*I am going through.*" we can look up with joy in our hearts when we say that phrase. The true meaning of the phrase *going through* simply means moving to get to the other side of your troubles. Let us look at Isaiah 43:2 (NIV Bible) to crystallize this concept of *going through* and how we are not alone. The verse reads:

"When you pass *through* the waters, I will be with you, and when you pass *through* the rivers, they will not sweep over you. When you walk *through* the fire, you will not be burned; the flames will not set you ablaze."

Remember, the Bible verse for this chapter is Psalm 48:14. For this God is our God forever. He will be our guide to the very end. Well, God and his Majestic Navigational Guiding System recalibrated my journey just like Siri sometimes will recalibrate your route to ensure that you get to your desired destination. I mentioned in Chapter One that God is the Master Builder, and we are his masterpiece. God will always be our guide, because he knows the plans he declared for each individual's life as he molds each of us into his masterpiece. I am so elated to follow God's Majestic Navigational Guiding System as I move through my life. I am filled with gratitude to have my lifelong friend Grace by my side every step of the way, magnifying God's amazing grace and mercy over my life.

Happy reflections and exploring <u>Your Story of Grace</u>.

CHAPTER THREE

Act Justly Love Mercy and Walk Humbly with Your God
(Micah 6:8) NIV Bible.

On my life journey, I have learned to lean hard on Micah 6:8 to stay on the path that God wants me to be on to honor him for all his grace, love, and mercy he has showered over my life, which is like a gentle, sweet rain and a warm glow of sunshine. Rain and sunshine are both needed for the myriad array of colorful flowers that blossom into a glorious picture in nature, and that picture is also us, my dear friends, to shine the beautiful light of God to the world. Yes, we have had sorrows, disappointments, and tears, but through it all, we keep holding on to God. We must continue to realize that God has given us the greatest gift anyone could ever give us, and that is the beautiful gift of salvation and grace, which are the keys to having a miraculous relationship with God the Father, Our Lord and Savior, and the Holy Spirit.

I want you to reflect on a scenario with me for a moment. Imagine that you have the most generous friend you have ever known, and he/she gives you the most outstanding and extraordinary gifts; money is never an option. Imagine your feelings right now. You are thinking about what gift I can give to my very dear friend. You begin to search through your mind what I can give my exceedingly kind and generous friend. Now, let us look at that same scenario from a spiritual standpoint view in the Bible verse John 3:16, which states, "For God so loved the world that he gave his one and only Son, that whoever believes in him shall not perish but have eternal life." The Bible verse John 3:16 shows us that God loves us so very much that he gave all humanity the greatest gift that anyone could ever give us, and that is the Gift of Salvation through his Son, Jesus Christ. We never have to wonder what we could give God for his spectacular Gift of Salvation. The Prophet Micah in the Bible verses Micah 6:7-8 gives us a perfect crystal-clear picture of what to offer God for his glorious gift and everlasting loving friendship. The offer is a beautiful roadmap for our journey of life, which is to act justly, love mercy, and always walk humbly with God.

I must say that my dear spiritual traveling guide, Grace, has truly enlightened me about these three important things God wants from us. Therefore, let us take a deeper look at the core things God wants from us. These three key elements of having pure actions of justice, mercy, and humility are essential to traveling the journey of God's plan and the gift he has placed within us as lights in the world.

Therefore, let us make sure we show God our gratitude by shining like the purest gold, honoring his request to humanity, which is to act justly, love mercy, and always walk humbly with God.

Happy reflections and exploring <u>Your Story of Grace</u>.

CHAPTER FOUR

My Grace Is Sufficient for Thee: For My Strength is Made Perfect in Weakness (II Corinthians: 12:9) KJV Bible

In this chapter, let us take a close look at the natural words sufficient and strength. Next, we will look at those two words through the lens of God's grace, God's strength made **perfect** to us in our weakness. The word sufficient means adequate for the purpose at hand. Whatever you need for the task at hand, when you have the gift of sufficiency on your side, you have what it takes. Now, the word strength means the very state of being strong and having unbending fortitude. The strength of fortitude is having firmness in mental, emotional, and physical endurance. This type of strength and fortitude demonstrates a never-give-up mindset of determination.

Now, let us take a look at the words sufficient and strength through the spiritual realm of God's magnificent **perfect** grace of heavenly favor that is free. If we can only believe that all things are possible with God when we are at our lowest point and void of strength to keep pressing forward in our natural life and spiritual life, God will step in with the spiritual realm of his grace that is absolutely perfect in our weakness as he provided for Paul. God provides us with flawless sufficiency and strength right in our most-weakest moment. In Isaiah 40: 28 – 31, we learn five key principles about God we need to cling to concerning the sufficiency and strength of his grace. The first principle is that God will not grow tired or weary. The second principle is that he gives strength to the weary and increases the power of the weak. The third principle is that if we hold to our hope in God, he will renew us with a heavenly realm of strength, not a manufactured strength. The fourth principle is that God will have us soar like eagles over any life storm; it should be known that eagles are the only birds that can fly over a natural storm. Finally, the fifth principle is that God will empower us with a heavenly realm of sufficiency and strength whereby we will run, not grow weary, walk, and not faint.

You see, metaphorically, we all have our personal thorn in the flesh. Paul beseeched God in II Corinthians 12:9 to remove his thorn from him, but God wanted to shine forth his glory through the sufficiency and strength of his grace that actually becomes **perfect** in our weakness. Honestly, I have had countless times I wanted God to remove a thorn/problem that I felt was too difficult for me to deal with, for example, my thorn of trauma, PTSD (Post Traumatic Stress Disorder), and depression.

Yes, christians can experience trauma, PTSD, and depression and should seek professional help for balance and wellness for our brain and emotions. It is not bad or weak to seek professional help for your mental illness and health; it is actually courageous for christians and all humanity. It is such a blessing when we are going through to know within our hearts that no matter how dark things look or feel, we know that we can hold to God's unchanging hand, because His grace is truly sufficient, and his strength is made **perfect** in our weakness. Grace my lifelong guide and guardian angel has taught me to acknowledge my weakness and my struggles with trauma, PTSD, and depression, and I can honestly say when I do acknowledge to God my struggles and need for help, I feel the compassion of God's grace just like the Bible verses in Lamentations 3: 22-23 tells us that God's mercies are new every morning and **great** is his faithfulness. So, when we

23

ever feel like Paul did in II Corinthians: 12:9 and begin to beseech God to remove our thorn(s) from us, that is the time to do what James 4:8 tells us in the Bible "Draw nigh to God, and he will draw nigh to you."

Let us always seek God's grace and mercy to guide us through this path and the journey of life. When we hit those thorns/problems, we can always rest in the Lord, knowing that his grace is sufficient, and his strength is made **perfect** in our weakness. It is very humbling to reflect on how God provides us with flawless sufficiency and strength of grace right in our weakest moments. I am also profoundly grateful for what First Peter 5: 6-7 instructs us to do concerning our thorns/problems, and that is to humble ourselves under the mighty hand of God and to cast all our cares upon him because he cares for us continuously.

Happy reflections and exploring Your Story of Grace.

Reflections and Lessons Learned in Chapter Four

CHAPTER FIVE

Now To Him Who Is Able to Do Exceedingly Abundantly
Above All That We Ask or Think, According to The Power
That Worketh in Us (Ephesians 3:20-21) KJV Bible

In this chapter, as you continue to journey with me in sharing <u>My Story of Grace</u>, I am so very elated to share what I consider to be one of God's greatest gifts of grace and the brightest diamond nugget next to giving the world his only beloved son to open up the door for salvation and everlasting life (John 3:16). The Bible verses Ephesians 3:20-21 are two of God's major diamond nuggets for experiencing his grace and mercy for our entire life journey right into eternal life everlasting. These two verses will guide us through our relationship and communication with our Heavenly Father. Think about it: God is letting us know here in Ephesians 3:20 that we have the power of his spirit working in us, and we will be filled with the abundance of his free gift of grace and favor. God clearly reveals to us that because we have his power of the Holy Spirit, he will do exceedingly and abundantly above *all* that we could ever ask of him or even imagine. Therefore, always remember that the gift of God's grace, mercy, and guidance is always free to us. Ephesians 3:20 was not just for the early church; Ephesians 3:21 reveals to us with certainty the great gift of grace in Ephesians 3:20 is for all generations and throughout all the world to the end of time and into eternity.

Think about and meditate on Ephesians 3:20-21 for five minutes. I would like you to stop reading at this point and meditate on those two verses for five minutes in an incredibly quiet place without any distractions. I recommend you to time yourself. I will do the same for five minutes of meditation, and then we will come back to the text. Okay, we are back after five minutes of meditations on Ephesians 3:20-21. Please reflect on your meditation at the end of the chapter in the reflection section. However, I will share my reflection during our five minutes of meditation on the two verses. I had an overwhelming reflection of how important it is for us to have the power in Ephesians 3:20 dwell and working in us in these current times. The early church had that power of the Holy Spirit working in them and they did great works and healed the sick. The word of God is always and forever true. Therefore, based on Ephesians 3:21 that same power should be working in our times. During our five-minute meditation, I started to give an account of all the times that God did abundant things in my life that was totally unimaginable. My heart and spirit were floating on a cloud of pure amazement.

During our time of meditation and reflection, I really took a look at the first part of Ephesians 3:20 concerning that God will give us what we ask for according to his will. Again, that is according to the power of the spirit that works in us. I really reflected on how I have been asking God to see the gift of healing for my love ones, friends, myself, and our land. In our world today we see serious illnesses physical and mental illnesses. We see the devastation of extreme weather and climate change. We also see extreme injustice, cruel hate, and vicious crimes. During our reflection about the two verses, I also realized that just because we do not **see** right now God granting what we are asking of him according to his will and the power of the Holy Spirit and faith working within us does not mean he is not working for us. God is always working for our good.

In Hebrews 11:1 the word makes it clear that we have a **Now** faith, which is the substance of things hoped for, and the evidence of things not seen. Therefore, Hebrews 11:1 is guiding us with God's grace and mercy to learn to wait patiently and hold to God's unchanging hand. My lifelong guide Grace helps me to not focus on what I cannot see, but to focus on God sees everything and that I must keep my hope and faith alive knowing that God can do exceedingly more than what I could ever think or imagine. Remember, this free gift of grace and favor is freely given to you and waiting for everyone who believes. I think it is very fitting to bring this chapter to a close with Psalm 34:8. The verse reads "O taste and see that the Lord is good: Blessed is the man that trusteth in him."

Happy reflections and exploring <u>Your Story of Grace</u>.

Reflections and Lessons Learned in Chapter Five

:

CHAPTER SIX

*Let Justice Run Down as Waters and Righteousness as A
Mighty Stream (Amos 5:24) KJV Bible*

I would like to start this chapter by taking a moment to
look at this majestic view. This splendiferous waterfall
relates to our core Bible verse for this Chapter Amos 5:24.
As an adult, I have developed a great affinity for reading
and studying Dr. Martin Luther King Jr. speeches and the
powerful gift of his oratorical skills.

Dr. Martin Luther King Jr. would use Amos 5:24 to let
humanity know that God's grace for justice and
righteousness is so mighty that it is like a mighty rushing
stream. As you look at the picture above you can see that

powerful waterfall. Now, visualize that is God's loving grace and mercy watching over us and making sure that his justice, protection, and righteousness will never leave us. God has promise in Isaiah 54:17 that no weapon or injustice turned against us will succeed. God is a keeper of all his promises. In Psalm 91: 1 God gives a promise that those who live in the shelter of the Most High will find rest in the shadow of the Almighty. If any injustice comes against us or any storms of life, God's grace and mercy will let his justice and righteousness run down as a mighty stream like the beautiful water fall above. All we have to do is to keep standing, trusting and wait patiently in God's grace, justice, and righteousness.

We know for sure that God is love. However, he is also a mighty God of justice just like Amos 5:24 depicts. I am sure that we have all experienced some form of injustice in our life that was very harmful. I have had a great deal of racial injustice against myself and my family. I was not judged by the content of my character, but instead I was judged by the color of my skin. My African-American and Native-American Cherokee ancestors going back to four generations suffered a great deal of injustice. My African-American ancestors experienced slavery and Jim Crow laws and rules in Mississippi. My father and my mother and their parents and siblings endured all the ugliness of Jim Crow. My Native-American Cherokee ancestors in the southeast stayed in the shadows of their beautiful Mother Earth Land against President Andrew Jackson's Indian Removal Act law. The Indian Removal Act Law was signed by President Andrew Jackson May 28, 1830, and it continued for decades until about 1860. However, there are still so many injustices to Native Americans. My Native-American Cherokee ancestors also stood up against the Trail of Tears, which was an act of genocide, because thousands of Cherokees died during the Indian Removal Act.

After studying and tracking primary sources and dates of birth not hearsay concerning my four generation of Cherokee grandmothers, I came to realize that my mother, my sister and I would not be here today if it was not for my fourth great Cherokee grandmother's bravery and her resilient warrior spirit; our ending would have never been our beginning of many generations of Cherokee warrior women. My fourth great grandmother was pregnant with my third great grandmother during the time of the Indian Removal Act and the trail of tears. This primary source information is based on my third great Cherokee grandmother's date of birth during the dates of the United States President Andrew Jackson's Indian Removal Act Law from May 28, 1830 - 1860. Cherokee women are warriors when it comes to their children and their land but mostly their children and that same warrior spirit runs through my blood and spirit even today.

I am profoundly grateful for my personal guide Grace. She has always given me a guiding light down the path of life helping me to see and know God's grace and mercy for me and all humanity. Whenever, I see all types of injustices that breaks my heart against any race of people, children, the poor, the homeless, the elderly, poor countries across the globe and all young and elderly people with mental health problems. I will always hold to my faith and hope in

Amos 5:24 to continue in pray that God's justice will run down as waters and righteousness as a mighty stream for all humanity. Therefore, take heart and always believe that God is a keeper of his promises. He will never leave you or forsake you no matter what injustices might come your way. Rest in the Lord and wait patiently in faith that God's mercy, grace, and justice is always on your side.

Happy reflections and exploring Your Story of Grace.

Reflections and Lessons Learned in Chapter Six

CHAPTER SEVEN

Put on the Whole Armor of God (Ephesians 6:10-18) KJV

EPHESIANS 6:10-18
"... Be strong in the Lord and in his mighty power. Put on the full armor of God so that you can take your stand against the devil's schemes." v. 10, 11

The Shield of Faith (Eph. 6:16)
Faith is being sure that God will keep His promises. Faith in God protects you when you are tempted to doubt.

The Helmet of Salvation (Eph. 6:17)
Put on the Helmet of Salvation by believing that Jesus Christ died for your sins and rose again.

The Breastplate of Righteousness (Eph. 6:14)
Righteousness is being honest, good, humble, and fair to others. It means standing up for weaker people.

The Belt of Truth (Eph. 6:14)
Truth keeps us from giving in to the world's beliefs. Compare your beliefs and actions to the truth of the Word of God.

The Sword of the Spirit (Eph. 6:17)
which is the Word of God. God's Word is our offensive weapon. When we tell others what the Bible says, the Holy Spirit helps people see their bad thoughts and actions, and makes them want to be forgiven.

Feet Prepared with the Gospel of Peace (Eph. 6:15)
The Gospel of Peace is being right with God and being contented in troubled times. Jesus said peacemakers were blessed.

THE ARMOR OF GOD

Imagine, the ancient warriors of the Roman Empire, Greek Empire and the Persian Empire concerning their training both physical and mental, the detailed armor they wore for battle and their absolute loyalty to their Empire and the safety of their Kingdom's rule and domination. The warriors' primary function was to uphold the high standing that their Empires would be the most powerful and superior in all the lands and other kingdoms. In Ephesians 6:10 -16 uses the example of Master Warriors of great Empires gear for great battles with the mission of conquering other Empires.

Our God Almighty has an Everlasting Kingdom, which is above all kingdoms and all authority. Therefore, the Mighty King of Glory gives us noticeably clear and explicit armor to symbolically wear to conquer and to have victory over every foe that seeks to rip us out of God's Kingdom. Now let's take a look at the armor that our Heavenly Father wants us to put on every day to maintain our salvation and to be a light for Jesus Christ to draw others to his redemption, love, mercy and grace.

Ephesians 6:10-18 King James Versions

"*10* Finally, my brethren, be strong in the Lord, and in the power of his might. *11*Put on the whole armor of God, that ye may be able to stand against the wiles of the devil. *12*For we wrestle not against flesh and blood, but against principalities, against powers, against rules of darkness of this world, against spiritual wickedness in high places. *13*Wherefore, take unto you the whole armor of God, that ye may be able to withstand in the evil day, and having done all to stand. *14*Stand therefore, having your loins girt about with truth, and having on the breastplate of righteousness; *15*and your feet shod with the preparation of the gospel of peace; *16*above all, taking the shield of faith, wherewith ye shall be able to quench all the fiery darts of the wicked. *17*And take the helmet of salvation, and the sword of the Spirit, which is the word of God: *18*praying always with all pray and supplication in the Spirit and watching thereunto with all perseverance and supplication for all the saints."

When we think about getting prepared for work, a birthday party, a special fancy dinner or a wedding, we all reflect very carefully and purposefully what exactly is the right thing to wear for the occasion. Therefore, it is imperative that we put on the whole armor of God to withstand the devil's plot to rip us out of **God's Mighty Kingdoms**. Our Heavenly Father's Kingdom is an everlasting Kingdom. God's sovereignty and dominion rules over everything and his loving and merciful Kingdom endures throughout all generations (Psalm 145:13 NIV). I have come to genuinely believe that the Lord's Pray in (Matthew 6:9-13) is a pray that we should pray every day to give all honor, praise, and our allegiance to our Heavenly Father who is the **King of Kings and the Lord of Lords**.

When we put on the whole armor of God and continue to **believe and trust** in the Power of God's Kingdom the word of God says that we are more than conquerors and that **nothing shall separate us** from the love of God, which is in Christ Jesus our Lord and Great Redeemer (Romans 8: 38-39 KJV). Our Heavenly Father's favor surrounds us like a shield (Psalm 5:12 NIV). He just wants us to put on daily the whole armor of God so that we can stand firm on God's love and powerful protection. The battle is already won. In Exodus 14:13-14, we are told to stand still and see the salvation of the Lord. He will fight for us; we will be able to hold our peace and rest in Jesus. He paid it all and all to him we are grateful with enduring love for giving us the greatest gift of all; he did not come down from the cross.

He gave is life for the pardon of our sins and to bring us into a new covenant relationship with our Heavenly Father for everlasting life. "For God so loved the world that he gave his only begotten Son, that whosoever believeth in him should not perish, but have everlasting life (John 3:16 KJV)."

Happy reflections and exploring <u>Your Story of Grace</u>.

CHAPTER EIGHT

Putting the Right Thoughts in My Gift Box of Thoughts
(Philippians 4:8) NIV

My journey of life with my guide, Grace, has helped me to draw from God's sustaining grace and to realize that my thought life is a splendiferous and powerful life force of positive energy wrapped up and gifted to me as an endless expanding *Gift Box of Thoughts*. The book of James 1:17 states: "Every good gift and every perfect gift is from above, coming down from the Father of lights, with whom there is no variation or shadow due to change." God's grace and mercy have taught me that what I allow my mind and heart to think about and dwell on will **shape my character, actions, decisions, and what comes out of my mouth for good or for bad.**

Philippians 4:8 is the core Bible verse for this chapter. It gives us a blueprint on how to think and what to think about. Once we take and utilize the blueprint for how to think and what to think on, our *Gift Box of Thoughts* from our Heavenly Father will become crystalized in all its brilliance for the Glory of God. Once, the *Gift Box of Thoughts* blueprint becomes actualized in our walk with God the Father, God the Son, and God the Holy Spirit we will start to develop a peace that passes all understanding and we will start to see the character of God in our actions, decision- making and the words that we speak.

Our world around us within our environment will also see the character of God within us demonstrating God's love, compassion, peace, and grace.

Our blueprint for thinking in Philippians 4:8 (NIV) states:

"Finally, brothers and sisters, whatever is true, whatever is noble, whatever is right, whatever is pure, whatever is lovely, whatever is admirable-if anything is excellent or praiseworthy-think about such things."

This chapter is very much needed for our daily lives as we utilize our *Gift Box of Thoughts* that God has given us to guide and shape our character and to transform us to agents of change for peace, love and joy for God's Magnificent Glory. My major goal is to develop my thoughts into having the mind of Christ Jesus. Philippians 2:5 states: "Let this mind be in you, which was also in Christ." I want to personally strive **on purpose** to have the mind of Christ Jesus every day so that the world might see the love of Heaven in my eyes and the likeness of our Lord Jesus Christ our Savior and Great Redeemer. Psalm 34:5a (ESV) states: Those who look to him are radiant."

Everything starts from our thought-life; that is why God gives us the wonderful *Gift Box of Thoughts* to be supported by the Holy Spirit to quicken and help us to develop the mind of Christ Jesus with his love, compassion, and mercy as we walk on our journey of life *demonstrating the presence* of God and that Immanuel is with us (Isaiah 7:14) in our sorrows and our greatest joy. It is imperative as children of God and Ambassadors of Jesus Christ to think on positive things in the Holy Spirit and to control our thoughts to have the Mind of Christ. I ask my guide Grace and the Holy Spirit to please help me to watch my thoughts, actions, decisions and what comes out of my mouth for good. Psalm 103:5 states: "Who satisfieth thy mouth with good things; so that thy youth is renewed like the eagle's."

I would like to share with you some extraordinary additional precious jewels from the Bible that can help us start to put God's word into our *Gift Box of Thoughts* every day. Imagine, every day waking up each morning to make the choice to embrace the positive mindset of the *Gift Box of Thoughts* from our Heavenly Father that he gives to us as children of God and of his glorious Kingdom. Remember, what we allow ourselves to think about can change our life. I turn to Jesus and my guide Grace who are the essence of God's loving grace, to help me with my daily walk with God to think on things above and to try my absolute best to stay and live in the presence of God. Here are some additional precious jewels Bible verses that you can add to your beautiful *Gift Box of Thoughts* each day.

1. Proverbs 4:23 (KJV) "Keep thy heart/mind with all diligence; for out it is the issues of life."
2. Isaiah 26:3 (ESV) "You keep him in perfect peace whose mind is stayed on you because he trusts in you."
3. Colossians 3:2 (AMP) "Set your mind and keep focused habitually on the things above [the heavenly things,] not on things that are on the earth [which have only temporal value.]"
4. Proverbs 18:21 (KJV) "Death and life are in the power of the tongue: and they that love it shall eat the fruit thereof." (i.e., the fruit of life and a positive mindset or the fruit of death and a negative mindset, which either mindset comes from the words that we speak and think)
5. Proverbs 23:7 (KJV) "For as he thinketh in his heart, so is he."

6. 2 Corinthians 10:4-5 (KJV) "For the weapons of our warfare are not carnal, but mighty through God to the pulling down imaginations/negative thinking, and every high thing that exalteth itself against the knowledge of God."

7. Ephesians 4:29 (KJV) Let no corrupt communication proceed out of your mouth, but that which is good to the use of edifying, that it may minister grace unto the hearers."

8. James 3:1-12 (KJV): "No man can tame the tongue."

9. Psalm 103:5 (KJV) "Who satisfieth thy mouth with good things; so that thy youth is renewed like the eagle's."

10. Proverbs 13:3 (AMP) "The one who guards his mouth [thinking before he speaks] protects his life. The one who opens his lips wide [and chatters without thinking] comes to ruin."

In the Book of James 3: 1-12 (KJV), James delineates that the tongue is an instrument of extraordinary power; it can bring about immense good and joy. However, on the other hand, the tongue can cause extreme pain, sorrow, and harm. It is the merciful and gracious God-given *Gift Box of Thoughts* that God freely gives us the choice to accept, whereby we can personally continue to fill our minds with positive thoughts, and the positive energy of God's love and grace will help us control our tongues, because as a man thinks so is he and it will come out through what we speak into the universe. In closing, I would like you to encourage us all to create our own beautifully decorated *Gift Box of Thoughts* to place our positive thoughts in using a small index card. Remember, think about the positive and weed out the negative.

Happy reflections and exploring Your Story of Grace.

Reflections and Lessons Learned in Chapter Eight

CHAPTER NINE

Grace Will Lead Me Home (II Timothy 4:18) NIV)

I have passed through many dangers, toils, and snares, and my guardian life-long angel Grace has walked with me through my life journey. My spiritual friend Grace has guided me throughout my life with God's merciful grace. I will continue to believe in faith that the Holy Spirit and my friend Grace, which is the, loving-kindness, and mercy of God the Father, God the Son, and God the Holy Spirit, have brought me safe thus far, and God's grace and my guardian life-long angel Grace will lead me home to the Glory of Heaven. My guardian angel and life-long friend Grace, who is present daily, ensures and symbolizes to me God's divine favor surrounding me like a shield. (Psalms 5:12: "Surely, Lord, you bless the righteous; you surround them with your favor as with a shield.") I am eternally grateful to my friend and guardian angel Grace for protecting me and guiding me throughout my journey of life with wisdom and shining God's love and forgiving mercy over me.

I am certain that Grace was assigned to me at birth. I feel her presence more than ever as I continue through my life's journey and my enduring love for God, Jesus, and the Holy Spirit; she is right with me, leading me home to heaven and the glory of God's presence. **I absolutely believe that the key Bible verse for this chapter, II Timothy 4:***18* *("The Lord will rescue me from every evil attack and will bring me safely to his heavenly kingdom. To him be glory forever and ever. Amen.")* is my guardian angel Grace's assignment to lead me safely home to my Heavenly Father. God's word is a lamp unto my feet and a light unto my path. (Psalm 119:105 KJV) and my guardian angel Grace holds that lamp (i.e., the Word of God) over me so that I can walk in the light of God's righteous path to help others see and experience the splendiferous, beautiful, and amazing love of God.

Dear friend, think of the most beautiful and amazing place or thing in the world. Now, imagine receiving the most **Amazing Free Gift** that is far more *precious* than the most *costly gift* that one could ever receive; the **Amazing Free Gift** is greater than *all* the money and land in the world. This **Amazing Free Gift** is the deepest enduring and unconditional love, grace, and mercy of God. John 3:16 (KJV) crystallizes all three elements mentioned, and they are deeply important. They are all interrelated with God's **Amazing Free Gift**, which is the gift of his son Jesus Christ, the Savior of the world from sin, that whosoever believes in Jesus and his sacrifice for salvation and redemption from sin will not perish but have everlasting life. God views us as his prize treasure, and he freely gives us his *free gift of grace and favor*.

I am so filled with gratitude for the gift of God's salvation and the grace and favor of our Mighty God over my life. The voices of a million angels could not express my gratitude to my Heavenly Father and the spiritual assignment of my dear friend and guardian angel Grace; she is truly amazing right from the **Throne of Grace** (Hebrews 4:16 KJV). In every situation that is good, joyous, beautiful, sad, depressive, or traumatizing, my guardian angel Grace is right there leading and guiding me with God's divine provision, divine acceptance, and divine approval of his grace and favor surrounding me with a shield (Psalm 5: 12 KJV).

My dearest friend, this love, grace, and favor is for all of humanity, and that means you. Therefore, Psalms 34:8 AMP states: "O taste and see that the Lord [our God] is good; How blessed [fortunate, prosperous, and favored by God] is the man who takes refuge in Him." I have tasted the glorious love, mercy, grace, and favor of God, and I have a deep assurance that my life-long guardian angel, Grace, will lead me home to the Glory of Heaven. I believe we all have a life-long guardian angel and the Holy Spirit to help us navigate our life journey with the enduring love of God's anointing to safely lead us home to heaven no matter what comes against us in this life.

Happy reflections and exploring Your Story of Grace.

Reflections and Lessons Learned in Chapter Nine

CHAPTER TEN

I Have Fought a Good Fight, I Have Finished My Course, I Have Kept the Faith (II Timothy 4: 7 - 8) KJV

In this last chapter, we will focus on God's amazing grace and mercy and how he guides us through this life into everlasting life. Psalm 48:14 states, "For this God is our God forever and ever: He will be our guide even unto death." We will take a deep look at the stages of our life and how we have three births. The first birth is when we are born into this earthly realm. Jeremiah 29:11, let us know by stating, "For I know the thoughts that I think of you, saith the Lord, thoughts of peace, and not evil, to give you expected end. **KJV Bible"** Now let us look at Jeremiah 29:11 in the **NIV Bible:** "For I know the plans I have for you, **Declares the Lord,** plans to prosper you and not to harm you. Plans to give you hope and a future."

Right from the start of our lives, God declared that he has a plan for us all; that plan is our life purpose and to believe and to accept Jesus Christ as our personal Savior. The Bible in John 3:16 states, **"For God so loved the world, that he gave his only begotten Son, that whosoever believeth in him should not perish, but have everlasting life."** Therefore, it is efficacious for everyone to seek God's plan and purpose for their individual life so that God's Seed of Greatness will be revealed in you to share your gift(s) to the world and to prosper in God's grace and mercy. I thank God for my Life Guide Grace and The Holy Spirit for leading and guiding me to live out God's plans for my life and to manifest my personal seed of greatness and the gifts that God had planned for me at birth. Today, I am living and walking out God's plan for my life and the gifts he has bestowed on me. God's plan and gifts of greatness is readily available to all humanity. **(Yes, That Means You Too.)**

It is essential that we apply John 3:16 to our personal life and accept Jesus Christ into our life as our personal Savior. This is the second birth into God's Kingdom of salvation and to be united with God's Holy Spirit to dwell within you. This is the second birth, which is the spiritual birth into God's Kingdom here on Earth. When we look at a grave marker, it states the day a person was born into the world, a natural birth. The little dash is not just a dash to depict the date of birth and the date of death. That dash signifies our life here on Earth; it is our **life lived**. Every day, when I awaken from sleep, I thank God for another day to live my dash/life to the fullest. I want his **Light** to shine through me and speak through me to help others realize the loyal, unending love of God and to experience God's unimaginable joy and his incredible peace, grace and mercy that is given to all that accept the Lord as their personal Savior. These are all a part of God's greatest gift to us throughout our second birth. Let us go back and reflect on this second birth, which is our dash or life lived.

When we live out our dash/life doing the will of God and helping others realize that the Bible verse John 3:16 is the Greatest Gift, and that God wants us to constantly ameliorate the gifts and purpose he placed over our life, that seed of greatness. Think about what it takes for a seed to grow into a flourishing, beautiful flower. Well, we must do the same thing to work out our seed of greatness, gifts, and talents that God has graced over our individual life to live out our dash, a life well lived.

Now, to the most glorious birth, the third birth, when someone reads the date of death, they must understand if a person has lived his or her dash by having accepted Jesus Christ as his or her personal Savior will have everlasting life in heaven. John 3:16 states, **"For God so loved the world, that he gave his only begotten Son, that whosoever believeth in him should not perish, but have everlasting life."** Therefore, we must all run our individual race/dash/life well to finish our course here on Earth and to begin our third birth into Eternal Life the Beginning of Everlasting life.

Therefore, let us look at Apostle Paul's statements concerning moving from the second birth into the eternal, everlasting, third birth. Paul states in II Timothy Chapter 4: 7-8 (KJV)

"I have fought a good fight, I have finished my course, I have kept the faith: henceforth, there is laid up for me a crown of righteousness, which the Lord, the righteous judge, shall give me at that day: and not to me only, but unto all of them also that love his appearing."

Therefore, it is a blessing to finish our *race/dash* here on Earth and move into the third birth of everlasting life.

Happy reflections and exploring Your Story of Grace.

Reflections and Lessons Learned in Chapter Ten

Dear reader, I hope you have enjoyed reading **My Story of Grace: A Self-Reflection Handbook** and your personal writing at the end of each chapter related to the connection of your personal story of God's amazing grace in your life. I sincerely hope the primary Bible verse for each chapter, and the reading of each chapter will illuminate your self-reflection on your journey with God's amazing grace. I leave you with the following Bible verse in Romans 15: 13 (NIV).

"May the God of hope fill you with all joy and peace as you trust in him, so that you may overflow with hope by the power of the Holy Spirit."

Blessings,

Dr. Edyth E. Young

Hebrews 13:20-21 — *"Now may the God of peace, who through the blood of the eternal covenant brought back from the dead our Lord Jesus, that great Shepherd of the sheep, equip you with everything good for doing his will, and may he work in us what is pleasing to him, through Jesus Christ, to whom be glory forever and ever. Amen."*